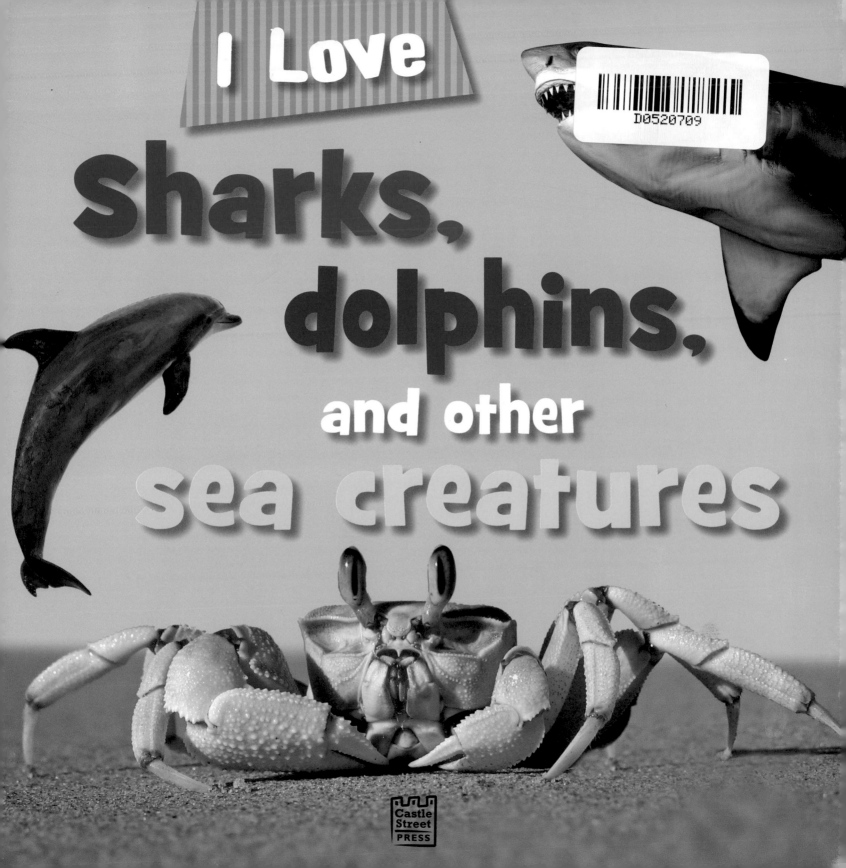

I Love
Sharks, dolphins,
and other
sea creatures

Castle Street PRESS

sharks

Sharks are amazing hunters of the sea! There are many different types of shark. Some have a **pointed** snout and **sharp** teeth while others have a **rectangular**-shaped head and **flat** teeth.

Bull shark

Whale shark

I love sharks

A shark's skeleton is made of cartilage instead of bone. Cartilage is lighter than bone. This helps the shark to stay afloat.

Bull sharks are powerful sharks that have even been spotted swimming in rivers.

The whale shark is the largest fish in the world. It can grow to be 68 ft (21 m) long – that's as long as a bus!

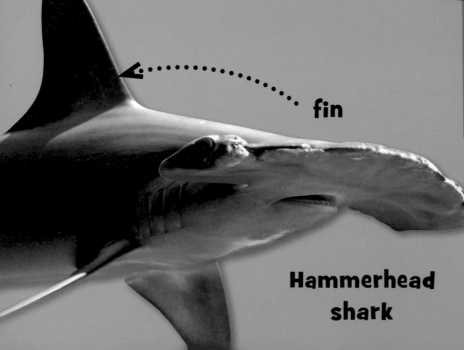

fin

Hammerhead shark

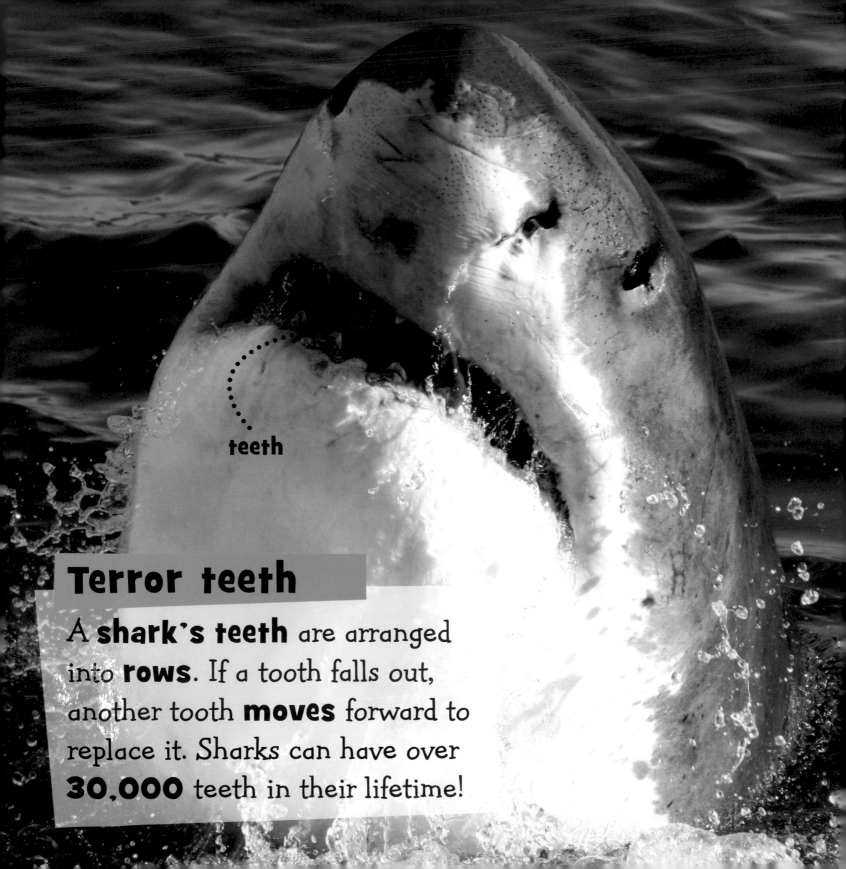

teeth

Terror teeth

A **shark's teeth** are arranged into **rows**. If a tooth falls out, another tooth **moves** forward to replace it. Sharks can have over **30,000** teeth in their lifetime!

Seals

Seals live all around the world. Some live in **Hawaii**, while others swim in the icy waters of **Antarctica!** Seals **feed** on fish, squid, crustaceans, and even other seals.

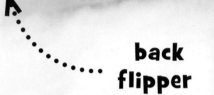

back flipper

Elephant seal

Leopard seal

I love seals

Many seals don't have ears!

For their size, seals have more blood in their body than any other mammal in the world.

The largest seals are the male elephant seals. They can be recognized by their trunk-like snout!

Leopard seals get their name from the spotted pattern on their coat.

Baby harp seal

fur

whiskers

front flipper

Brilliant blubber

Seals have a **thick** layer of **fat** called **blubber** under their skin. This helps to keep them **warm** when they are in **cold** water.

Whales

Whales are the largest and **heaviest** animals in the world! They swim using their large flippers and **tail**, and can swim deep down to great **depths**.

Sonic songs

Whales make lots of different **sounds**. The humpback whale's **songs** are made up of **moans**, **clicks**, **cries**, and **howls** and can last for up to half an hour!

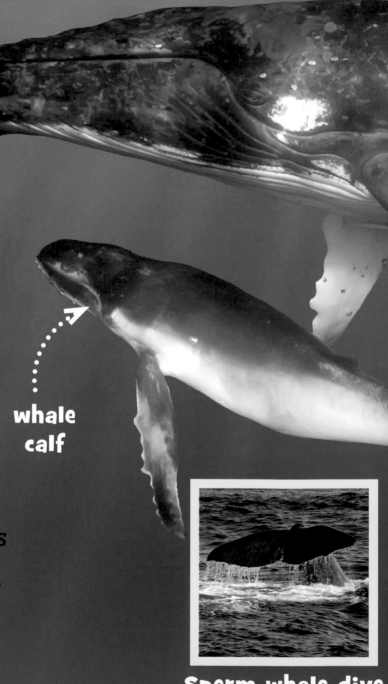

whale calf

Sperm whale dive

tail

flipper

blowhole

I love whales

We do not have to think about breathing, but whales actually have to remember to breathe!

The blue whale makes the tallest blow of water out of its blowhole. The blow can reach up to 50 ft (15 m) high!

Sperm whales can dive deeper than any other whale. One was recorded reaching a depth of 6,560 ft (2,000 m).

Dolphins

dorsal fin

Dolphins are **intelligent** and playful animals that belong to the **whale** family. They are excellent swimmers – some can even **jump** out of the water and spin around in the air!

Killer size

Killer whales are the largest animals in the dolphin family. The **dorsal fin** on top of their body can grow to 6 ft (1.8 m) – that's as **tall** as a **man!**

Bottlenose dolphin

beak

flipper

Killer whale

flukes

I love dolphins

Killer whales have been recorded swimming as fast as 34 mph (55.5 kph)!

Spinner dolphins have been seen jumping high into the air and spinning around up to seven times!

A dolphin's two tail flippers are called flukes.

Dolphins travel together in small groups called pods. Pods have been known to help an injured dolphin reach the surface.

pod of dolphins

Jellyfish

Jellyfish have a **soft** body and lots of tentacles. The **tentacles** are covered in tiny **stings**, which they use to **stun** and kill their prey.

bell

Mediterranean jellyfish

tentacle

oral arms

I love jellyfish

Some jellyfish glow in the dark!

A jellyfish is made up almost entirely of water.

Jellyfish have no heart, no bones, no eyes, and no brain!

The cassiopeia jellyfish floats upside down and is sometimes called the upside-down jellyfish.

Medusa jellyfish

Cassiopeia jellyfish

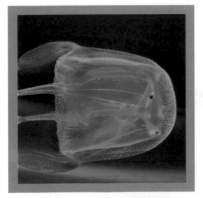

Box jellyfish

Deadly jelly

The **box** jellyfish is one of the most **dangerous** animals in the world. Its sting can kill a human.

Crabs

Crabs belong to a family called **crustaceans**. When a crab grows too big for its **shell**, it splits the shell open and grows a new one.

Hermit crab

eye

claw

Cracking claws

Crabs use their strong **claws** to crack shells and tear their food. They also use them for show and to **defend** themselves.

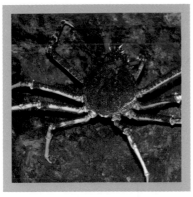

Japanese spider crab

I love crabs

Crabs' eyes are on stalks.

The Japanese spider crab is the largest crab. It measures almost 13 ft (4 m) across when its legs are stretched out.

Hermit crabs don't have a hard shell, so they use other animals' shells instead.

Crabs can run sideways!

leg

sideways walk

Squids

Squids move quickly through the water by **sucking** water into their body and **forcing** it out again like a **jet propeller**. They have eight arms and two longer **tentacles** to grab their prey.

eye

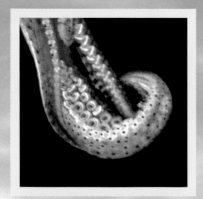

tentacles

I love squids

Squids eat using their parrot-like beaks!

The giant squid and the colossal squid are thought to have the largest eyes of any living animals!

Squids have two hearts!

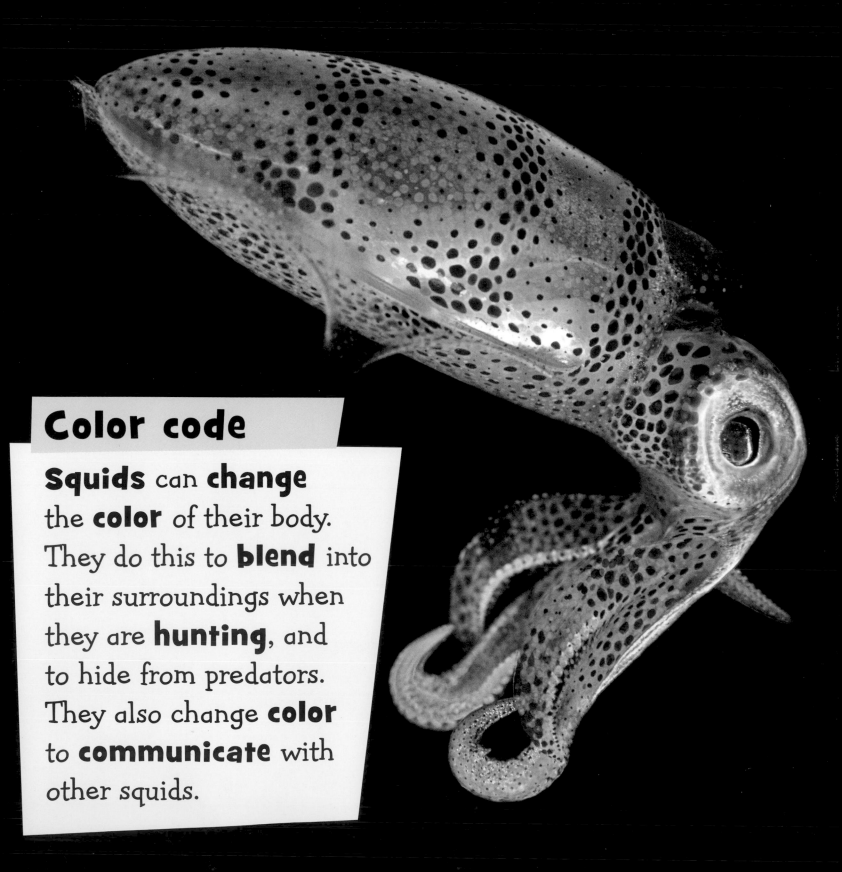

Color code

Squids can **change** the **color** of their body. They do this to **blend** into their surroundings when they are **hunting**, and to hide from predators. They also change **color** to **communicate** with other squids.

Sea turtles

hard shell

Sea turtles are **reptiles**. They have a hard **shell** that protects them from attackers and flipper-like legs that they use to swim. They often swim a **long** way to find food and mate. This journey is called a **migration**.

Loggerhead turtle

flipper

Green turtle

I love sea turtles

Turtles can hold their breath for a long time. One loggerhead turtle was recorded diving for 10 hours!

It is thought that turtles can sleep underwater.

Female green turtles lay the most eggs of any sea turtle in one season. They lay up to 1,100 eggs!

Baby leatherback turtle

Hot hatching

Leatherback turtles produce **male** or **female** hatchlings depending on the **temperature** of their nest. A **cooler** temperature means they will produce **males** and a **higher** temperature means they will produce **females**.

Gone fishing!

Guess who?

Look at the pictures, read the clues, and guess what each one is.

1  I use my strong claws to crack shells and tear my food.

2 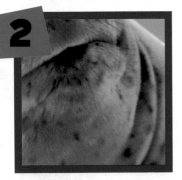 I have a thick layer of fat to keep me nice and warm.

3 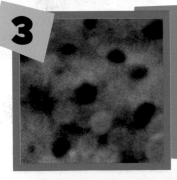 I have two hearts, eight arms, and a parrot-like beak.

4 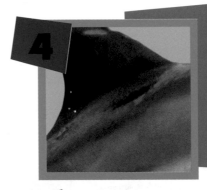 I like traveling with my friends in small groups called pods.

5 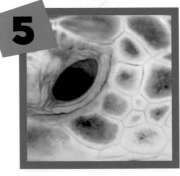 I can hold my breath for a long time, and I even sleep underwater.

6  I am the largest fish in the world and can grow to 68 ft (21 m) long.